★ It's My State! ★ ★ ★ ★ ★

ILLINOIS

The Prairie State

Claire Price-Groff, Elizabeth Kaplan, Gerry Boehme

Cavendish
Square

New York

Published in 2015 by Cavendish Square Publishing, LLC
243 5th Avenue, Suite 136, New York, NY 10016

CPSIA Compliance Information: Batch #WWS15CSQ

Price-Groff, Claire.
Illinois / Claire Price-Groff, Elizabeth Kaplan, Gerry Boehme. — Third edition.
pages cm. — (It's my state!)
Includes index.
ISBN 978-1-50260-011-0 (hardcover) ISBN 978-1-50260-012-7 (ebook)
1. Illinois—Juvenile literature. I. Kaplan, Elizabeth. II. Boehme, Gerry. III. Title.

F541.3.P75 2015
977.3—dc23

2014026351

Editor: Fletcher Doyle
Senior Copy Editor: Wendy A. Reynolds
Art Director: Jeffrey Talbot
Designer: Joseph Macri
Senior Production Manager: Jennifer Ryder-Talbot
Production Editor: David McNamara
Photo Research by J8 Media

ILLINOIS ★ ★ ★ ★ ★

CONTENTS

State Tree: White Oak

Young Illinoisans chose this acorn-bearing tree as their state tree in 1973. In the fall, the tree's leaves change color, creating a beautiful display of orange, red, and yellow.

State Bird: Cardinal

In the past, these brightly colored birds visited the state only in spring and summer. Today, they are year-round residents.

State Fish: Bluegill

Easy to spot because of the bluish color of its gills, the bluegill became the state fish in 1986. Bluegills can be found throughout the state. These small sunfish are only about 9 inches (23 centimeters) long but are a very popular fish to catch.

ILLINOIS
POPULATION: 12,830,632

Population Data: U.S. Bureau of the Census, 2010

★ State Insect: Monarch Butterfly

Schoolchildren proposed this orange-and-black butterfly as the state insect in 1974. The monarch butterfly's bold color is actually a warning to other animals that it would make a very bad-tasting meal.

★ State Fossil: Tully Monster

About 300 hundred million years ago, this soft-bodied sea animal thrived. First discovered by Francis Tully in 1958, Tully monster fossils are all over Illinois—more than a hundred have been found.

★ State Snack: Popcorn

Native Americans in Illinois started growing corn about 100 CE. Many farmers in Illinois still grow corn today, and more than three hundred farms grow popping corn. Popcorn became the official state snack food in 2003 due to a proposal made by second- and third-grade students and their teacher from Cunningham Elementary School in Joliet.

The beauty of Illinois is captured in the Springbrook Prairie Nature Preserve.

The Prairie State

I llinoisans like to think of their state as the center of the nation's heartland. In different parts of the state, ancient cypress swamps and majestic river cliffs fill the landscape. You might see riverboats gliding over the smooth waters of the major rivers that pass around and through Illinois. You can find peaceful prairies with rolling fields of wheat and herds of grazing cattle. Also running through this heartland are many highways and roads that lead from the farmland toward the big cities and their surrounding areas, called suburbs. From bustling cities to quiet prairies, Illinois seems to have it all.

Illinois looks kind of like a giant key. It is the twenty-fourth largest state and covers 55,584 square miles (143,962 square kilometers). The state has 102 counties. Chicago, the state's largest city, is in Cook County. It has the second-highest population of any county in the United States. Springfield, the state capital, is in Sangamon County in the central part of the state.

The Landscape

There are different types of terrain in the northwestern section of the state. That is where you will find Illinois' highest points and deepest valleys. Jagged limestone cliffs and rocky outcrops break up hilly prairies. The northwestern portion of the state also has wetlands and forests.

Chicago sits on the shores of Lake Michigan.

Northeast Illinois has rich plains dotted with small lakes and marshes. Much of the farmland that once covered the region has given way to cities. Chicago is located in the eastern section of those plains. The southern end of Lake Michigan serves as the northeastern border of the state.

The central portion of Illinois boasts some of the most fertile soil in the United States. Flat land covers much of the area, perfect for farming. However, gently rolling hills also add variety to the landscape. The hills were created millions of years ago when glaciers—large bodies of ice—moved across the earth, bringing rich soil to the region. The glaciers also carved high ridges, deep canyons, and caves across south central Illinois. The soil in the south central part of the state, however, is mostly clay and is not good for farming.

The western portion of Illinois, between the Illinois and Mississippi rivers, has many hills,

ILLINOIS BORDERS

North:	Wisconsin
	Lake Michigan
South:	Kentucky
	Missouri
East:	Indiana
	Lake Michigan
West:	Iowa
	Missouri

valleys, small lakes, and streams. This west central area of the state is perfect for people who love fishing, boating, and mountain biking. Many miles of trails have been developed to help people enjoy that sport.

The wind has carved interesting rock formations in the 300-million-year-old Garden of the Gods.

To the south are the Illinois Ozarks, a hilly region with impressive sandstone cliffs and deep canyons. Unlike the level central landscape, glaciers did not create this rugged terrain. The Shawnee National Forest stretches across the region, covering more than 250,000 acres (101,170 hectares). The only national forest in Illinois, it is a popular place for hiking, camping, canoeing, and horseback riding. Within the Shawnee National Forest is the Garden of the Gods wilderness area. Large rock formations, sculpted by the wind into interesting shapes, give this part of the forest its name. Hikers in the Garden of the Gods can see rocks in unusual shapes, including a camel, a mushroom, a smokestack, and a table.

Two large rivers, the Ohio and the Mississippi, bound the southern part of the state. This region is sometimes called Egypt, or Little Egypt. One explanation for these nicknames is that the majestic rivers made early European American settlers think of the Nile River in Egypt. The southernmost city in Illinois is Cairo (in Illinois pronounced "CARE-oh"), which is named after that famous Egyptian city.

Waterways

Rivers and lakes abound in Illinois, and several bodies of water form some Illinois borders. The Mississippi River cuts western Illinois into a series of notches as it flows south. Lake Michigan, one of the five **Great Lakes**, sits at the state's northeast corner. The Wabash River separates southeastern Illinois from Indiana. The Ohio River forms the border between southern Illinois and Kentucky. The Illinois River drains a large area

ILLINOIS
POPULATION BY COUNTY

County	Population	County	Population	County	Population
Adams County	67,103	Henry County	50,486	Piatt County	16,729
Alexander County	8,238	Iroquois County	29,718	Pike County	16,430
Bond County	17,768	Jackson County	60,218	Pope County	4,470
Boone County	54,165	Jasper County	9,698	Pulaski County	6,161
Brown County	6,937	Jefferson County	38,827	Putnam County	6,006
Bureau County	34,978	Jersey County	22,985	Randolph County	33,476
Calhoun County	5,089	Jo Daviess County	22,678	Richland County	16,233
Carroll County	15,387	Johnson County	12,582	Rock Island County	147,546
Cass County	13,642	Kane County	515,269	St. Clair County	270,056
Champaign County	201,081	Kankakee County	113,449	Saline County	24,913
Christian County	34,800	Kendall County	114,736	Sangamon County	197,465
Clark County	16,335	Knox County	52,919	Schuyler County	7,544
Clay County	13,815	Lake County	703,462	Scott County	5,355
Clinton County	37,762	LaSalle County	113,924	Shelby County	22,363
Coles County	53,873	Lawrence County	16,833	Stark County	5,994
Cook County	5,194,675	Lee County	36,031	Stephenson County	47,711
Crawford County	19,817	Livingston County	38,950	Tazewell County	135,394
Cumberland County	11,048	Logan County	30,305	Union County	17,808
DeKalb County	105,160	McDonough County	32,612	Vermilion County	81,625
De Witt County	16,561	McHenry County	308,760	Wabash County	11,947
Douglas County	19,980	McLean County	169,572	Warren County	17,707
DuPage County	916,924	Macon County	110,768	Washington County	14,716
Edgar County	18,576	Macoupin County	47,765	Wayne County	16,760
Edwards County	6,721	Madison County	269,282	White County	14,665
Effingham County	34,242	Marion County	39,437	Whiteside County	58,498
Fayette County	22,140	Marshall County	12,640	Will County	677,560
Ford County	14,081	Mason County	14,666	Williamson County	66,357
Franklin County	39,561	Massac County	15,429	Winnebago County	295,266
Fulton County	37,069	Menard County	12,705	Woodford County	38,664
Gallatin County	5,589	Mercer County	16,434		
Greene County	13,886	Monroe County	32,957	Total State Population	12,830,632
Grundy County	50,063	Montgomery County	30,104		
Hamilton County	8,457	Morgan County	35,547		
Hancock County	19,104	Moultrie County	14,846		
Hardin County	4,320	Ogle County	53,497		
Henderson County	7,331	Peoria County	186,494		
		Perry County	22,350		

The Mississippi and Ohio rivers meet at Cairo.

Shaped by the Wind

The Shawnee National Forest is the only national forest in Illinois. It is a popular place for hiking, camping, canoeing, and horseback riding. Within the Shawnee National Forest is the Garden of the Gods wilderness area. Large rock formations, sculpted by the wind into interesting shapes, including a camel, a table, and a mushroom, give this part of the forest its name.

across the central portion of the state. Almost all the rivers in Illinois, large or small, eventually flow into the Mississippi. Many of these rivers are great for fishing, which is popular throughout Illinois.

Illinois' most important port city is Chicago on Lake Michigan. Lake Michigan is the sixth-largest freshwater lake in the world. A person standing on its shore cannot see across it to the opposite side. Illinois has several other large lakes, including Carlyle Lake and Rend Lake. Many large lakes in Illinois were created when a dam was built across a river.

Illinois' lakes and rivers are important both to the state's economy and to its wildlife. Commercial boats and barges commonly carry farm products and manufactured items to Illinois' ports. The goods are then shipped to the rest of the country and all over the world. Pleasure and fishing boats also cruise the lakes and rivers. Many types of birds, fish, and other wildlife make their homes in the state's waterways.

Climate

Long, cold winters and hot, humid summers are common in northern Illinois. Almost every year, Chicago newspaper headlines report illnesses or deaths related to weather extremes.

In the winter, it is common for the temperature to dip well below 0 degrees Fahrenheit (–17 degrees Celsius). In the summer, it is equally common for the temperature to rise well above 90°F (32°C).

In the spring and early summer, the Mississippi and other rivers in Illinois sometimes overflow, causing floods in the lowlands along the rivers. In 1993, thousands of people in

When the Mississippi River flooded in 2008, farms such as this one in Quincy were wiped out.

Caterpillar Headquarters

Lincoln Tomb

The Ledge

1. Cahokia Mounds State Historic Site

Collinsville's **Cahokia Mounds** is the largest prehistoric Native American settlement north of Mexico. Many **artifacts** have been found there. Its 120 mounds include the 100-foot-(30.5 meter) high Monks Mound, the largest prehistoric earthwork in the Americas.

2. Caterpillar Visitors Center

Based in Peoria, Caterpillar is a leading manufacturer of construction and mining equipment, engines, turbines and locomotives. The Peoria visitors' center includes simulators that show what it's like to operate Caterpillar equipment.

3. Lincoln Tomb

After President Abraham Lincoln was **assassinated** in 1865, his remains were returned to his hometown of Springfield. The Lincoln Tomb was built between 1869 and 1874 in Oak Ridge Cemetery and is the final resting place of President Lincoln, his wife and three of their four children.

4. Magnificent Mile

A stretch of downtown Chicago's North Michigan Avenue has gained worldwide fame for offering hundreds of stores, restaurants, hotels and many entertainment choices. Known as the "Magnificent Mile," it runs thirteen blocks from the banks of the Chicago River north to Oak Street.

5. Skydeck Chicago's The Ledge

Skydeck Chicago's The Ledge is located on the 103rd floor of Chicago's Willis Tower, the second-tallest building in the Western Hemisphere. The Ledge's glass boxes jut out from the side of the skyscraper, offering great views.

ILLINOIS ★ ★ ★ ★

Super Museum

Grant's Home

Wrigley Field

6. Starved Rock State Park

Located in Utica, Starved Rock State Park includes seasonal waterfalls, awe-inspiring bluffs and rugged canyons. Hiking trails work their way through towering trees and scenic overlooks along the Illinois River. Outdoor activities include hiking, cross-country skiing, trolley rides, fishing, and picnicking.

7. Super Museum

The Super Museum in Metropolis, Illinois, features a collection of Superman memorabilia, including more than twenty thousand items relating to the Superman saga, from his first appearance in comic books to recent movies.

8. Ulysses S. Grant Home

After he led the Union Army to victory in the Civil War, a group of Galena citizens presented the General with a furnished house on Bouthillier Street in his hometown. Now fully restored to the 1860s time period, it contains many of Grant's personal belongings.

9. Wildlife Prairie State Park

Located in Hannah City, Wildlife Prairie State Park is home to more than 150 animals that are native to Illinois, including wolves, bison, black bear, elk, and cougars. The Adventure Trek Tour includes a trip through the bison and elk pasture.

10. Wrigley Field

Built in 1914, Wrigley Field has hosted baseball for 100 years and is the second oldest major league ballpark behind Boston's Fenway Park (1912). The Chicago Cubs have played in Wrigley since 1916.

Water Crossroads

Chicago is the largest inland general cargo port in America. The Saint Lawrence Seaway and the Great Lakes meet the Illinois and inland waterway system at Chicago. The city is the beginning and the end of barge traffic between the Seaway, inland points, and the Gulf of Mexico through the Illinois, Mississippi, Missouri, Ohio, and the Arkansas rivers.

the western part of the state lost farms, homes, and businesses to floods. The flooding was the worst in Illinois history. Severe flooding again occurred on the Mississippi and other rivers throughout central Illinois in 2008.

In the spring of 2013, four inches of rain fell around Galesburg in only thirty minutes, causing flooding that shut down Carl Sandberg College for several days. The water was high enough to cause desks to float, and up to thirty computers were damaged.

Severe thunderstorms are not uncommon in Illinois. With these storms comes the threat of tornadoes, especially in the spring and summer. A tornado is a swirling column of air that stretches from a storm cloud all the way to the ground. In a tornado, wind speeds can reach more than 200

Winters in Chicago can be ice-cold.

miles per hour (320 kilometers per hour). Tornadoes can form quickly and uproot trees, rip off roofs, and toss cars into the air.

Despite the sometimes harsh weather, Illinoisans love to watch their state change with the seasons—the burst of new life in spring, the full bloom of summer, the glorious colors of fall, and the beauty of freshly fallen snow in winter.

Wildlife

Farm crops grow well in Illinois but so do many wildflowers, grasses, and trees. Purple violets, lilies, bluebells, hyacinths, marsh marigolds, and other wildflowers sprinkle the roadsides and fields with color in spring and summer.

In the past, more than half the state was covered with forests of ash, cottonwood, elm, hickory, and oak. Today, only about 12 percent of Illinois land is forested. European

The floor of the Ryerson Conservation Area in Riverwoods is lushly covered.

Reduced habitat has hurt populations of the yellow-headed blackbird.

American settlers who plowed the land and planted crops cut down more than two-thirds of Illinois' original forests. Other forests were cleared to build towns and cities. Today, the most heavily forested part of the state lies in the south, within the Shawnee National Forest.

Some farmers in Illinois are planting trees for forests and wild grasses for prairies. Much of the land had been seriously eroded, or worn away, when it was farmed. One farmer described the gullies on his farm as deep enough to completely hold a car. Now this land is being managed to attract and feed wildlife. In addition, replanting the land with native grasses and trees helps prevent water pollution and flooding.

A variety of animals and birds are native to Illinois. The white-tailed deer—the state's official animal—is the biggest animal in Illinois. Rabbits, squirrels, muskrats, skunks, raccoons, foxes, and mink scamper through the forests. Ducks, quail, grouse, and pheasant nest and feed along the state's waterways and in fields. Huge flocks of Canada geese darken the skies in the spring. They return from a winter spent farther south and stop in Illinois to build nests, lay eggs, and hatch their young. Thousands of Canada geese also live year-round throughout the state. The birds create problems by destroying crops and fouling lakes and ponds. However, they are a protected species and can be hunted only during specific times of the year.

Many birds make their homes in the trees of Illinois. Cardinals and other songbirds sing out from the treetops. Bald eagles watch for prey while perched on high.

Threatened Wildlife

Some animals that were once common in Illinois have become extinct. The yellow-headed blackbird is in danger of disappearing from the state. Many of the marshes and wetlands that are the home of this beautiful bird have been drained. People have planted crops and built houses and factories on the drained land.

Other animals are in danger of dying out. Among them are fish, including several species of sturgeon and chubs. Types of turtles, snakes, and salamanders could also completely disappear. Pollution and the loss of forests have put species of hawks, owls, songbirds, and shore birds, and several small woods and prairie animals, at risk of losing their natural homes. Many other animals and numerous plants are endangered in Illinois and are likely to become extinct unless people make a strong effort to save them.

Eastern Red Bat

Fox Squirrel

1. Bobcat

Weighing up to 40 pounds (18 kilograms), this cat is named for its short, "bobbed" tail that is only about 5 inches (12.7 cm) long. For many years the Illinois bobcat population was very low, but numbers have grown since the 1990s.

2. Coyote

Coyotes usually hunt at night, roaming an area as wide as 30 miles (48 km). They are swift runners, reaching speeds of more than 40 miles per hour (64 kilometers per hour). That is faster than the speed limit on most Illinois city streets.

3. Eastern Red Bat

The tiny red bat weighs less than 1 ounce (30 grams) and is one of twelve kinds of bats found in Illinois. The red bat gets its name from its brownish-red fur. Each hair has a white tip, so this bat could easily be nicknamed the frosted bat.

4. Fox Squirrel

The fox squirrel is the largest tree squirrel in Illinois. It lives mostly at the edge of forests or woodlands. It is good at moving from tree to tree and can jump nearly 18 feet (5.5 meters).

5. Goldenglow Flower

There are not many woodland flowers that will reach the height of this coneflower. These brilliant-yellow, daisy-like flowers dot Illinois roadsides in midsummer.

Goldenglow Flower

6. Northern Cardinal

Cardinals are the Illinois state bird. They live in Illinois throughout the year and have become quite abundant since 1900, when they were considered rare in the northern part of the state. The males are bright red, the females a dusty reddish-brown.

7. Purple Violet

There are several varieties of the purple violet, Illinois' state flower. The most common of these, the dooryard violet, is one of the most recognizable native wildflowers in the state and also one of the most easily grown.

8. Turkey Vulture

Turkey vultures are large soaring birds that people often mistake for eagles. They are becoming more common in central Illinois. Turkey vultures are grouped in with birds of prey but are more closely related to herons and storks.

9. White-Tailed Deer

The white-tailed deer is the only native species of deer in Illinois. The upper throat, belly, inner rump, and insides of the legs are white, as is the underside of the tail, thus the name. Typically only males grow antlers.

10. Wild Blue Iris

These beautiful flowers bloom in early spring. The flowers contain three blue petals and three blue sepals with a yellow base. In Illinois, they can be found along the shores of ponds and small lakes, in marshes, and in wet parts of prairies.

Purple Violet

Turkey Vulture

Corn grows abundantly in the fields of Illinois.

From the Beginning

What do the frozen plains of Siberia in northern Asia have to do with Illinois? Scientists believe that between ten thousand and thirty thousand years ago, the Bering Sea—the stretch of water between Alaska and eastern Siberia—did not exist. Sea levels were lower then, and land that is now under the Bering Sea was above water, creating a land bridge between the two continents. Most anthropologists (scientists who study different cultures, including ancient cultures) think a few brave, strong people crossed that bridge. If this is true, the many Native tribes that spread across the Americas are the descendants of those adventurers.

The earliest people to live in the area now called Illinois were **nomadic** groups that moved from place to place hunting large game. Later, people who lived in the region hunted smaller game and gathered wild grains and edible roots, bulbs, berries, and nuts. Eventually, the region's Natives began to grow grain instead of gathering it where it grew wild. They ground the grain into coarse flour for cooking and baking.

The First Settlements

Over time, ancient people in what is now Illinois learned more about the food plants whose seeds they collected and scattered each year. They learned where the plants grew

23

best and decided to stay in these areas year-round. About three thousand years ago, they began building permanent settlements, mostly in river valleys.

The ancient Illinoisans, even before they built year-round settlements, buried some members of their groups in earthen mounds. Over the centuries, they built larger and more complex mounds. By about 100 BCE, mound building had become an important part of the culture of many peoples living in the American Midwest.

Cities on the Mississippi

About 700 CE, people in Illinois began growing corn as a main food source. It was a more reliable source of food than other crops. The cultivation of corn led to growth in the population and to the development of a distinctive culture. Because most of the people lived along the Mississippi or other rivers flowing into the Mississippi, the culture is called the Mississippian culture.

This is an illustration of Monks Mound, which was part of the Cahokia civilization.

In Mississippian culture, small villages surrounded large towns or cities. At the center of most towns and cities was a large, flat mound with a temple or a leader's home built on top. The largest of the Mississippian cities was Cahokia, in southwestern Illinois. The city served as a cultural center for centuries. About twenty thousand people lived in Cahokia when the city was at its peak.

Over the next 250 years, Cahokia's population declined. By 1400, very few people lived in Cahokia and in other large Mississippian villages in present-day Illinois. This may have been because the climate was getting colder, which led to poor harvests. Overpopulation, disease, and invasion might have also added to the problems.

The First European Settlers

In 1673, the French government in New France (part of present-day Canada) was looking

Louis Jolliet and priest Jacques Marquette explored from Lake Michigan south down the Mississippi River.

The Native People

When Europeans first arrived in the Great Lakes region, two Native American tribes inhabited the land that would eventually become the state of Illinois. The first group, known to the French explorers as the Illinois, or Illiniwek, was a collection of several independent Native American tribes that spoke a common language, had similar ways of life and shared a large section of the central Mississippi River valley, including most of what is today Illinois. These tribes included Kaskaskias, Cahokias, Tamaroas, Peorias, and Metchigamis. The second group was known as the Miami tribe, and they lived in villages located south and west of Lake Michigan. The Shawnee and Chickasaw lived in small parts of the southern region, and the Dakota and the Ho-Chunk the northern borders of what is now Wisconsin.

Both the Illinois and Miami tribes spoke a language in the Algonquian language family called "Miami-Illinois." Although they pronounced some words differently, Miami and Illinois peoples could easily understand one another. They made canoes of hollowed-out logs, and used dogs as pack animals to transport their goods. (There were no horses until European settlers brought them.)

In the seventeenth century, the Illinois suffered from exposure to infectious diseases brought by the Europeans, to which they had no natural immunity. They also faced warfare due to the expansion of the Iroquois tribe into the eastern Great Lakes region. During the

A Native American family lives across from Kinzie House, which was near Fort Dearborn.

1700s and early 1800s, the territory of the Illinois tribe shrank and the Miami tribe moved eastward. Many of the Illinois migrated to present-day eastern Kansas to escape the pressure from other tribes and encroaching European settlers. Other tribes then moved to the Illinois area to take over that land. These newly arrived tribes included the Fox (Mesquakie), Ioway, Kickapoo, Mascouten, Piankashaw, Potawatomi, Sauk, Shawnee, Wea, and Winnebago. Most of these tribes disappeared from Illinois by about the mid nineteenth century, either through warfare or resettlement to other territories by the federal government.

There are no federally or state-recognized Native American tribes in Illinois today. The Native American tribes of Illinois still exist, but like many other native tribes, they were forced to move to **reservations** by the American government. The Peoria Tribe of Oklahoma is made up of people indigenous to Illinois.

The Illinois

The Illinois were a populous and powerful nation that occupied a large section of the Mississippi River valley. They became important allies of French fur traders and colonists who came to live among them.

Houses: The Illinois moved between three types of settlements during the year. During the spring and summer, they raised corn and lived in mat-covered longhouses near rivers. In June and July, they built hunting camps in the prairies using bark-covered lodges. For the winter, they moved to areas along the bottoms of dry rivers that were good locations for hunting. They lived in oval, mat-covered lodges called wigwams.

Clothing: The early Illinois wore clothing made from the skins and hair of bison, deer, and other animals. As time passed and they became more dependent on French trade goods, the Illinois began to replace their traditional clothing with garments made of wool and other fabrics.

Music: The main Illinois musical instruments included the drum, rattle, and flute. Drums were made from large ceramic pots with an opening covered by buckskin. Rattles were fashioned from a hollow gourd that contained glass beads and was attached to a wooden handle. Flutes were carved from wood.

Children: Illini children did chores but also played with toys and games such as child-sized bows and arrows and corn husk dolls. Illini teenagers also liked to play a version of lacrosse and other sports. Illini mothers, like many Native Americans, traditionally carried their infants in cradleboards on their backs.

for new trade routes. Louis Jolliet and Jacques Marquette were chosen to explore the river that the Algonquian-speakers called *Misi sipi*, or "big river." They wanted to see if the river stretched west to the Pacific Ocean. Louis Jolliet was a French Canadian who had been exploring the Great Lakes region for New France. Jacques Marquette was a French priest who had worked and lived among the Native Americans and could speak a number of Native American languages. In May 1673, Marquette and Jolliet launched canoes at the northern edge of Lake Michigan and began their journey southward.

Marquette and Jolliet paddled along the shores of Lake Michigan and then traveled down rivers in what is today Wisconsin. They eventually reached the Mississippi River. They followed it as far south as present-day Arkansas. They also traveled north, along the Illinois River. A year later, Marquette returned to the banks of the Illinois River to establish a mission (a religious settlement) at a Native American village called Kaskaskia, which later became the town of Utica.

The French claimed the area that Marquette and Jolliet explored, naming it Illinois, after the Native Americans who lived there. In the early 1700s, the French considered

The British surrender one of their forts to George Rogers Clark.

Illinois part of their province of Louisiana—a vast area that included nearly the entire midsection of North America. The first permanent European settlement in Illinois was established in the town of Cahokia in 1699.

Despite their differences, Europeans and Native Americans traded with each other. Native Americans exchanged animal skins for the Europeans' metal tools, horses, and guns. However, the European settlers also pushed Native Americans off the land and brought new diseases to North America. Native Americans had never been exposed to these illnesses and had no resistance to them. As a result, Native Americans died by the thousands.

The arrival of more Europeans took its toll on the land. Settlers chopped down forests and hunted animals for food and their skins. Native Americans could no longer find the animals they needed for food. In self-defense, they learned to use their horses and guns to fight back against the Europeans. More European colonists kept coming, however, and the Native Americans were fighting a hopeless battle.

The European settlers also fought each other. During the French and Indian War (1754–1763), the British and French competed for control of North America and both were aided by Native American allies. The British won the war and gained control of Illinois and most other French territory in North America east of the Mississippi River. Despite this, most white people in Illinois at that time were French.

The American Revolution

By the 1770s, many colonists along the eastern coast of North America wanted to break free from British control. The original thirteen colonies approved the Declaration of Independence on July 4, 1776, but freedom did not come easily. First, the colonists had to fight and win the American Revolution.

Most battles were fought in the eastern colonies, but some fighting took place in Illinois. The most important battle was on July 4, 1778. American forces led by George Rogers Clark captured the British forts at Kaskaskia, Cahokia, and several other small towns. In his journal Clark wrote, "In the evening, we got within a few miles of the town, where we lay until near dark. . . . In a very little time we had complete possession." Clark claimed all the territory north of the Ohio River as part of the newly formed United

Making a Corn Husk Doll

Wherever corn was grown as a crop, children in both Native American and Colonial American families used husks to fashion dolls. Follow these simple instructions to create your own unique doll.

What You Need

9–12 pieces of fresh (green) corn husk, reserving silk for hair

Strong string

Water

Paper towels/newspaper

Scissors

Glue

What To Do

- Take four cornhusks and arrange them by placing one on a flat surface, two side by side on top of the first, and then one more on top of the two. The top and bottom husks should be aligned, with parts of the middle two sticking out the sides.

- Using a small piece of string, tie the straight ends together tightly.

- Trim and round the edges with scissors. Trim off the pointed ends.

- Turn upside down and pull long ends of husks down over the trimmed edges.

- Tie with string to form the "head."

- Take another husk, flatten it, and roll into a tight cylinder.

- Tie each end with string. This forms the doll's arms.

- Fit the arms inside of the long husks, just below the "neck."

- Tie with string, as shown, to form a "waist."

- Drape a husk around the arms and upper body in a crisscross pattern to form "shoulders."

- Take four or five husks, straight edges together, and arrange around waist. These form a "skirt" for the doll.

- Tie with string.

- If desired, form legs for the doll by splitting the skirt evenly into two bunches and tying each bunch together at the bottom and at the knees. Trim them so they are equal in length. Finish the doll by tying small strips of husk around the neck and waist to hide the string. Glue the silk to the head for hair. Small scraps of cloth may be used to dress the doll.

States. Clark's victory at Kaskaskia also persuaded local French residents to fight on the American side.

The Illinois Territory

When the American colonists eventually won their independence from Britain in 1783, almost all the land between the former colonies and the Mississippi River became part of the new United States. The area north of the Ohio River, including Illinois, was called the Northwest Territory. In 1800, the part of the Northwest Territory that included present-day Illinois was renamed the Indiana Territory. Nine years later, the district split. Part

Black Hawk of the Saux and Fox tribes was admired for his dignity in defeat.

of the district became the Illinois Territory, which included present-day Illinois, Wisconsin, and Michigan.

In the early 1800s, Americans of European descent started moving into present-day Illinois in large numbers. The new land was good for farming, so they built cabins and chopped through the tough prairie sod (grass-covered soil) to plant crops. Many items these settlers had taken for granted in their previous homes were not available. They had to make most of their own goods or do without them.

Illinois officially became the twenty-first state on December 3, 1818. By 1830, the state's population had grown to more than 160,000 people.

As more settlers arrived, the remaining Native Americans were forced to move west. Some Native Americans refused to leave their homelands. In 1832, Black Hawk, a leader among the Sauk and Fox tribes, tried to take back tribal land in northern Illinois and Wisconsin. He and his warriors fought bravely, but they were badly outnumbered and were quickly defeated. President Andrew Jackson sent Black Hawk and his son Whirling Thunder around the country as "trophies" of war. The two men behaved with such dignity that they gained much admiration. Black Hawk returned to his people on a reservation in Iowa, where he wrote his autobiography.

Throughout the period, the United States government signed pacts and treaties with Native tribes. The government took away the lands on which the Indians had always lived and gave them other land farther west. But as European-American settlers moved toward the Pacific coast, many of those treaties were broken.

The Civil War

By the mid 1800s, tensions between the Northern and Southern states were rising. The Northern states flourished as a result of manufacturing, trade, and mass production. The Southern states thrived by farming cash crops, such as cotton, tobacco, and rice. Southern plantation owners relied on black slaves to raise their crops and slavery was a basic part of Southern life.

As the United States grew, adding territory in the West, the nation became divided over the issue of slavery. The Northern states were "free states." Slavery had been abolished or was never legal in these states. The free states wanted slavery to be illegal in most of the new states that were added as the nation grew. In addition, some people opposed slavery on moral grounds. They wanted slavery to be abolished throughout the nation.

The Southern states were "slave states." Not only did they consider it a right to own slaves, they also tended to vote together in Congress and did not want to lose influence in the national government as new states were added. To help hold on to their political power, the slave states wanted slavery to be legal in western territories. At the least, they wanted the territories to vote on whether their new state would be a free state or a slave state. By the spring of 1861, eleven Southern states had broken away from the Union (the United States) and formed the Confederate States of America. The Civil War had begun.

Illinois was a free state and was one of the twenty-three states that fought for the Union against the Confederacy during the Civil War. More than 250,000 Illinoisans fought in the Union army. Nearly thirty-five-thousand of these soldiers died in the war.

Abraham Lincoln debates Stephen A. Douglas at Knox College in Galesburg.

10 KEY CITIES ★ ★ ★

Chicago

Aurora

Joliet

1. Chicago: population 2,695,598

The third-largest city in the United States, Chicago sits on the shore of Lake Michigan. While the city itself has more than 2.6 million people, the surrounding area ("**Chicagoland**") contains nearly ten million people in three states—Illinois, Wisconsin, and Indiana.

2. Aurora: population 197,899

Located on the western edge of Greater Chicago, Aurora has grown impressively over the past half century. It is known as the "City of Lights," because it was one of the first cities in the United States to implement an all-electric street lighting system in 1881.

3. Rockford: population 152,871

Located halfway between Chicago and Galena, the community was also briefly known as "Midway." Thousands of Swedish **immigrants** settled in Rockford between 1835 and the early 1900s and their history is still celebrated today.

4. Joliet: population 147,433

Once an industrial city, Joliet's economy entered a period of decline in the late 1970s and 1980s. Joliet's economy rebounded in the 1990s, and now millions of people visit its riverboat casinos, drag racing, and NASCAR tracks.

5. Naperville: population 141,853

Considered to be a western suburb of Chicago, Naperville was once known for farming and manufacturing but has evolved into an affluent city. In 2012, Naperville was listed on CNN Money magazine's Top 100 Best Places to Live.

6. Springfield: population 116,250

Springfield is located in the mostly flat plains of central Illinois. It serves as the state capital and the state government is the city's largest employer. Springfield is also the final resting place of President Abraham Lincoln.

7. Peoria: population 115,007

Peoria was the site of the first European settlement in Illinois. French fur traders arrived in the Peoria River Valley in 1673. French explorers built a small fort in 1680, which was the first European building in the Midwest.

8. Elgin: population 108,188

Elgin was founded in 1836 and has been known as a center for dairy farming and as the leading producer of fine watches in the United States. It began to grow again in the 1990s with the arrival of the Grand Victoria riverboat casino.

9. Waukegan: population 89,078

The industries of Waukegan, located on the shore of Lake Michigan about 40 miles (64 km) north of Chicago, faced economic challenges in the last decades of the twentieth century. Today, it is an attractive urban community focused on revitalizing its waterfront.

10. Cicero: population 83,891

The town of Cicero is bordered on the north and east by Chicago and is the suburb nearest to downtown. Cicero has the only town form of government in Cook County, and is governed by a board of trustees.

Springfield

Peoria

Elgin

Abraham Lincoln strived to preserve the Union.

One Illinois soldier who fought in the war was Ulysses S. Grant. He volunteered in Springfield and rose in rank to become the head of the Union army. A few years after the war ended, in 1868, Grant was elected president of the United States.

Abraham Lincoln was a central figure before and during the Civil War. Having studied and practiced law in Illinois, Lincoln set his sights on a political career. While running for the U.S. Senate in 1858, Lincoln participated in many debates in the state against Stephen A. Douglas and argued against slavery. He lost the Senate election to Douglas but, in 1860, Lincoln was elected president of the United States. He was reelected in 1864.

Fort Dearborn was built on the south side of the Chicago River in 1803.

Lincoln believed that the Union must be held together. In a famous speech on June 17, 1858, during the Senate race, he said: "A house divided against itself cannot stand. I believe this government cannot endure permanently half slave and half free. I do not expect the Union to be dissolved; I do not expect the house to fall; but I do expect it will cease to be divided. It will become all one thing, or all the other."

He led the country through the Civil War and is often thought of as one of America's greatest leaders. However, Lincoln did not get to continue his leadership after the Union victory. On April 14, 1865, only a few days after the main Confederate army surrendered, Lincoln was shot while watching a play in Washington, DC. He died the next day. On April 21, a funeral train left Washington, DC, and made its way through 180 cities and seven states before arriving in Springfield, Illinois. Lincoln was buried there on May 4. A few months after Lincoln's death, the U.S. Constitution was changed. The Thirteenth Amendment officially ended slavery throughout the United States.

Illinoisans are extremely proud that Abraham Lincoln spent most of his adult life in Illinois. Like many people around the world, they admire Lincoln's principles. It is no surprise then that Illinoisans adopted "Land of Lincoln" as the state's slogan.

The historic Water Tower survived the Great Chicago Fire and became a symbol for the city's citizens.

Growth and Industrialization

Today, Chicago is one of the largest cities in the United States. But when the first European explorers arrived there in the late 1600s, the site was a swampy area where wild onions and garlic grew. They used a Native American word, *Checagou*, which, some settlers have written, meant "skunk" or "stink onion."

In 1803 the U.S. Army established Fort Dearborn near present-day Chicago. Soon, European American settlers started coming to the area. In

The Great Chicago Fire destroyed eighteen thousand buildings.

1812, Native Americans attacked and burned Fort Dearborn. The fort was rebuilt four years later, but few people returned to the settlement until the Sauk tribe's leader, Black Hawk, was defeated in the early 1830s. From then on, the city grew rapidly. New canals connected Chicago, along with other growing cities, to the rivers that fed into the Mississippi. Railroads were built across the continent. Many of these train lines met in Chicago. The canals and the railroads helped Chicago become an important port and industrial center in the mid 1800s.

Improvements in machinery have made farms much more productive.

But Chicago almost did not survive into the 1900s. On the night of October 8, 1871, a fire started in or near Patrick and Catherine O'Leary's barn in Chicago and spread through the city. Legend says that a cow kicked over a lantern, but no one knows for sure how the fire started. The Great Chicago Fire destroyed nearly every home and business in the city. More than three hundred people died and eighteen thousand buildings were destroyed, leaving many people homeless. The people of Chicago fought back, and soon the city was on the rise again. One of the buildings to survive the fire was the Historic Water Tower. It still stands today, surrounded by soaring skyscrapers, and serves as a symbol of Chicago's strong spirit.

Shopping by Mail

Today's shoppers buy many products from online stores on the Internet, but the idea of shopping without actually going to the store is not new. In the 1800s, shoppers from all over the country ordered everything from underwear to water pumps from catalogs that came in the mail, which still happens today.

Chicago residents gather to protest economic conditions during the Depression.

World War II put people to work at the airplane engine factory in Melrose, where whites and African Americans toiled side by side.

New Industries in Illinois

During the 1800s, many new industries were born in Illinois. Many of these companies still exist today.

Cyrus McCormick invented a reaper that helped farmers harvest huge fields of crops quickly. John Deere invented a steel plow to replace old wooden and iron plows. The steel plows worked better than wooden ones in the tough prairie soil and lasted longer. Farmers from Illinois and neighboring states sent cattle and hogs to be slaughtered, or killed, in stockyards near Chicago, and Gustavus Swift opened a meat-processing plant in the area. Aaron Montgomery Ward began a mail-order business. He was so successful that Richard Sears and Alvah Roebuck did the same thing. Both companies opened large department stores that generations of shoppers loved to visit. Although Ward's company went out of business after more than 125 years, Sears still has many department stores.

Chicago's factories were so successful that by 1890 Illinois was the third-largest manufacturing state in the nation. Products included farm machinery, clothing, steel products, food products, and more.

Two World Wars

In 1914, World War I broke out in Europe. The United States entered the war in 1917, joining Great Britain and France in fighting Germany and Austria-Hungary. Illinoisans contributed to the war by enlisting in the armed forces and by working in factories to produce war materials.

In the 1930s, the nation sank into the **Great Depression**. Thousands of banks closed and businesses failed. Many people lost their farms or their jobs and some lost their homes. Millions of people across the country were unemployed. It was a time of great hardship.

By the end of the 1930s, the world was drawn in to World War II. In Europe, Adolf Hitler's Nazi German troops stormed across neighboring countries. In Asia, Japan conquered parts of China and numerous territories that at the time were European colonies. The United States entered the war in late 1941, after the Japanese bombed Pearl Harbor, the site of the U.S. naval base in Hawaii.

Factories and farms scrambled to provide supplies needed by the armed forces, including weapons, tanks, trucks, ships, planes, uniforms, and clothing. The war helped to ease the unemployment of the Great Depression. Thousands of men and women from Illinois served in the armed forces. Many more served by working in factories and on farms as the economy had to ramp up to produce the products needed to supply the troops.

The war brought about great advances in atomic research. In 1942, under the direction of Enrico Fermi, an Italian American physicist, scientists at the University of Chicago set off the first human-made **nuclear** chain reaction. A nuclear chain reaction involves the release of tremendous energy from the nucleus (center) of an atom, the building block of matter. More research led to the creation of the atomic bomb. The United States dropped two atomic bombs on Japanese cities, which helped bring World War II to an end in 1945. Nuclear research also led to peaceful uses of nuclear power for power plants that make electricity. Today, the Chicago area remains a leader in atomic and nuclear research.

Illinois Today

During the second half of the twentieth century, Illinoisans faced many problems. Increasing costs forced many farmers to sell their land to large corporations or to land developers. Land that was once rich farmland was cleared to make way for homes, businesses, and factories.

Urban areas also faced rough times. During the 1900s, cities had grown more crowded, leading to increases in racial tension, poverty, crime, and drug problems. By the mid- and late 1900s, many people and businesses moved out of the cities into the expanding suburbs. Inner cities had less money to support their schools and for upkeep of older neighborhoods. Inner-city residents also had fewer opportunities to find good jobs.

But Illinoisans today are working hard to solve those problems and create a bright future. Immigrants from all over the world, especially from Latin America and Asia, have moved to Illinois. They are helping to make Illinois a diverse and successful state.

The suburbs around Chicago grew in the 1950s.

10 KEY DATES IN STATE HISTORY

1. **10,000-8,000 BCE**

Paleo Native Americans roam the area now called Illinois, living in small camps and subsisting on large game and wild plants.

2. **May 17, 1673**

Marquette and Jolliet set out from Lake Michigan to explore part of present-day Illinois.

3. **February 10, 1763**

The French and Indian War between Great Britain and France ends. The British win and claim the area that includes Illinois.

4. **December 3, 1818**

Illinois becomes the nation's twenty-first state.

5. **April 9, 1865**

The Great Chicago Fire destroys most of the city. Historians agree that the Chicago Fire did indeed start that night in the barn of Mr. and Mrs. Patrick and Catherine O'Leary, but the exact cause is still unknown.

6. **October 14, 1908**

The Chicago Cubs become first major league baseball team to win back-to-back World Series. As of the 2014 season, the Cubs had not won a World Series since.

7. **May 5, 1973**

The Sears Tower in Chicago is completed. At the time, it was the world's tallest building. (The building was officially renamed the Willis Tower in 2009.)

8. **November 3, 1992**

Illinois voters elect Carol Moseley-Braun to the U.S. Senate. She becomes the first African American woman elected to the Senate.

9. **November 4, 2008**

Illinois senator Barack Obama becomes the first African-American to be elected president of the United States. He won a second term in 2012.

10. **February 22, 2011**

Former White House chief of staff Rahm Emanuel was elected the fifty-fifth mayor of Chicago.

Illinois presents
its residents with
many opportunities
for recreation.

The People

Illinoisans live in cities, suburbs near those cities, country towns, and on farms. They work in a wide variety of jobs. Some people can trace their family history in Illinois back many generations. Others are newcomers to the state.

Farming Life

Farm life in Illinois today is much different from when the first settlers came. Today, most farms are fully computerized, and modern machinery makes farm life easier than it used to be. However, farm families still work hard. Children get up about 5:00 a.m. to do chores before getting on the school bus.

Illinois farmers and their families are not isolated or behind the times. Today, with computers and Internet connections, people who live in rural areas can enjoy some of the same benefits of modern life as city people.

From Country Towns to Small Cities

Although more than three-quarters of Illinois is still made up of farm fields, most Illinoisans live in the towns and small cities sprinkled throughout the state. Each place has its own history, style, and culture. Galena in northwestern Illinois is a beautiful, old, historic town. Carbondale claims a nationally recognized university. Decatur, in

Who Illinoisans Are

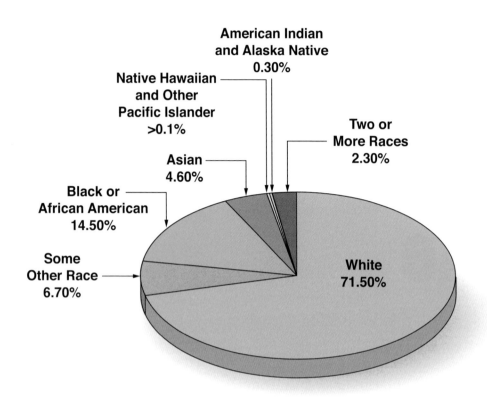

Total Population
12,830,632

American Indian
and Alaska Native
0.30%

Native Hawaiian
and Other
Pacific Islander
>0.1%

Two or
More Races
2.30%

Asian
4.60%

Black or
African American
14.50%

White
71.50%

Some
Other Race
6.70%

Hispanic or Latino (of any race):

• **2,027,578 people (15.80%)**
Note: The pie chart shows the racial breakdown of the state's population based on the categories used by the U.S. Bureau of the Census. The Census Bureau reports information for Hispanics or Latinos separately, since they may be of any race. Percentages in the pie chart may not add to 100 because of rounding.

Source: U.S. Bureau of the Census, 2010 Census

the middle of Illinois, is a center for business and industry and an urban hub for the surrounding farming areas. Some cities in Illinois are part of a bigger metropolitan area, which has a large central city surrounded by smaller cities or towns.

Every ten years, the U.S. government counts the number of people living in the United States. This count is called the census. According to the 2010 Census, Illinois is home to more than 12.8 million people.

The biggest metropolitan area in Illinois is Chicago. People who live there refer to the city and surrounding suburbs as Chicagoland. Chicago has about 2.7 million people, making it the third-largest city in the country. Like many large cities, Chicago has interesting restaurants, creative theater, and museums filled with fascinating exhibits. Chicago is also known for its beautiful lakefront, its stunning architecture, and for being the home of Second City, a renowned sketch comedy troupe. In different seasons, people can go hiking, biking, canoeing, kayaking, swimming, sailing, and cross-country skiing, all in downtown Chicago. Bustling with activity, many parts of Chicago are great places to live and work as well as to visit.

However, not all parts of the city are quite so well off. In poor neighborhoods, many people have to deal with problems such as high unemployment and crime rates, overcrowding, and poverty. Some public schools in Chicago are very crowded. They do not have enough money to provide textbooks or even teachers for all their students.

To address problems such as these, students in some of Chicago's high schools have been working with parents and community groups to improve their education. They did a yearlong study to find out why many students in the local public schools do not complete high school. They visited successful urban schools in other cities to learn effective ways to teach and motivate students. The students produced a report that they presented to the city. Their report outlined how they could work with the community and the school system to help more students graduate from high school and go on to college.

Education gets the attention of Illinoisans.

Many of Chicago's suburbs offer the benefits of both a large city and a smaller town. Many people like living in the suburbs because they can live in a quiet and peaceful area but still be close to the liveliness of the city.

Diversity in Illinois

As of 2010, the population of Illinois was more than 12.8 million. Only four states had more people. Though more than 70 percent of the population is white, the state's residents come from a wide range of countries and cultures. Illinoisans also come from many different religious backgrounds. The largest religious groups are Protestants and Catholics. The state is also home to many Jews, Muslims, Hindus, and Buddhists. Some Illinoisans choose not to be part of any organized religion.

Illinois is important in the history of the Church of Jesus Christ of Latter Day Saints,

Gwendolyn Brooks

Sandra Cisneros

Miles Davis

1. Jane Addams

An important early social reformer who spoke out against child labor and worked for world peace, Addams was born in 1860 in Cedarville, Illinois. In 1889, she co-founded Hull House, a settlement house where immigrants could take classes and get help.

2. Gwendolyn Brooks

A renowned poet, Brooks was born in Kansas in 1917, but she grew up in Chicago. Many of her poems are about the experiences of African Americans. Appointed Poet Laureate of Illinois in 1968, she died in Chicago in 2000.

3. Sandra Cisneros

Born in 1954, Cisneros wrote her first book in the Chicago neighborhood where she grew up. *The House on Mango Street* is a bestseller, read in many classrooms. Her foundation gives a yearly writing award.

4. Hillary Clinton

Born in Chicago, Hillary Clinton graduated from Yale Law School before serving as First Lady during her husband Bill Clinton's presidency. Clinton was later elected U.S. Senator from New York before serving as U.S. Secretary of State under President Barack Obama.

5. Miles Davis

Born in Alton, Illinois in 1926, this world-famous trumpet player, bandleader, composer, arranger and producer is considered to be one of the most influential jazz musicians in history. Miles Davis has been called "the master of cool."

Walt Disney

Betty Friedan

Oprah Winfrey

6. Walt Disney

Born in Chicago in 1901, Walt Disney went on to create Mickey Mouse and many other much-loved cartoon characters. Disney died in 1966, but his characters live on.

7. Betty Friedan

Born in Peoria, Friedan was a major leader of the feminist movement during the 1960s and 1970s. She co-founded the **National Organization for Women (NOW)** and became its first President.

8. Adlai E. Stevenson II

The son of a former vice president was elected governor of Illinois in 1948. As the Democratic National Committee's presidential candidate, he lost to Dwight D. Eisenhower in 1952 and 1956. A founder of the United Nations, he served as chief U.S. delegate from 1961 until his death in 1965.

9. Dwyane Wade

Born in 1982 in the south side of Chicago and nicknamed "D-Wade" and "Flash," Wade has played for the Miami Heat since 2003, winning his first championship in 2006 before teaming with fellow stars LeBron James and Chris Bosh to win again in 2012 and 2013.

10. Oprah Winfrey

Born in Mississippi and residing now in California, Winfrey will always be linked to Chicago, where she moved in 1984 to host the morning TV show *A.M. Chicago*, which went national. In 2013, Winfrey was awarded the Presidential Medal of Freedom.

America's Main Street

Route 66 is one of America's most legendary roads. Starting in Chicago and running all the way to Los Angeles, it was called the "Main Street of America" because it wound through small towns across the Midwest and Southwest. Route 66 was bypassed section by section as the high-speed Interstate highways were completed.

or the Mormons. In 1839, founder Joseph Smith and his followers settled in Commerce, Illinois. Smith renamed the city Nauvoo. The city's population grew to about twelve thousand. Still, the Mormons were often persecuted for their beliefs. Smith was murdered in jail in Carthage, Illinois, in June 1844. Less than two years later, Brigham Young led the Mormons out of Nauvoo to a new settlement in Utah. Today, the city of Nauvoo attracts many visitors who come to see historic Mormon sites.

Native Americans make up less than one percent of the population of Illinois. Despite their small numbers, Native Americans have a strong presence in the state. For decades, they have worked to fight stereotypes and give people accurate information about their different tribes, their cultures, and their traditions. For example, many college athletic teams are named after Native American

Farmers' markets allow small growers to sell their produce.

tribes or chiefs. The team names were not meant to offend anyone, but the team symbols and mascots often failed to show respect for native cultures. Native Americans and others at the University of Illinois at Champaign-Urbana brought national attention to this issue. Over the years, athletic events at the school featured the university mascot, Chief Illiniwek. The mascot would do a dance to raise team spirit. That presented several problems. The Illinois natives (also called the Illiniwek) were Algonquian. But the mascot's costume was based on the clothing of the Plains Indians. Even more important, traditional dances are sacred rituals in Native American cultures. They are not meant to entertain crowds at athletic events. Chief Illiniwek's dance offended many people.

Two Native Americans carve a totem pole to be displayed at the Field Museum in Chicago.

In 2007, after numerous meetings with native groups, faculty, students, and alumni, the University of Illinois retired Chief Illiniwek as the school's mascot.

A First for African Americans

The first African American town to be incorporated in the United States was Brooklyn, Illinois. Brooklyn, which was first named Lovejoy, had its beginnings in the 1820s. Black slaves escaped to the area and set up a community of farmers and craftspeople. Brooklyn, Illinois, remained a destination for African Americans for decades.

Today, most African Americans in Illinois do not live in small towns like Brooklyn. More than 97 percent of the state's African Americans live in urban areas. Since the early 1900s, they have formed organizations to promote education and help people find jobs. The Urban League is one example.

African Americans in Illinois have formed other organizations to help children and families make good lives for themselves. In Chicago, Rockford, and Bloomington, the organization 100 Black Men coordinates mentoring and other programs for African-American children, especially young boys. A mentor is an older or more experienced person who works one-on-one with a younger person and acts as a role model. Members of 100 Black Men groups generally have successful careers. When they meet with students, they talk about things that have helped them set and reach their goals: self-respect, taking responsibility, being part of a healthy community, and education.

Many African American Illinoisans have made significant contributions to the arts. Gwendolyn Brooks was the first African-American poet to win a Pulitzer Prize—a major award for authors, poets, journalists, and composers. Miles Davis (jazz), Mahalia Jackson (gospel), and Muddy Waters (the blues) each helped popularize a different style of music and, in doing so, enriched American culture. Music producer Quincy Jones helped create many famous recordings, including Michael Jackson's *Thriller* album. Popular talk show host Oprah Winfrey gained her fame in Chicago. She has used her show to influence people in many positive ways. Oprah has also used her wealth and power to start charities and to highlight problems in society. With Oprah's Book Club, she has promoted reading and helped sell millions of books.

Other Large Ethnic Groups

Over the past thirty years, many immigrants have moved to Illinois. For example, since the early 1980s, thousands of people from Eastern Europe have come to the state. In fact,

Derek Rose of the Chicago Bulls teaches young players at a basketball clinic.

Chicago, which has a large Polish-American population, claims to be the world's largest "Polish city" outside Poland.

Large numbers of people from Latin America and Asia have also moved to Illinois in recent decades. Hispanic Americans come to Illinois from many different places: Mexico, Puerto Rico, Venezuela, El Salvador, Colombia, and Guatemala, to name just a few. Asian Americans also come from a wide variety of countries, including India, the Philippines, China, South Korea, Vietnam, and Japan.

Immigrants often play an important part in shaping

Immigrants bring their native foods to the United States.

their communities. Some immigrants open stores and restaurants that sell their native foods and goods. The growth of immigrant populations can lead to problems, however. Sometimes residents do not welcome the changes in their communities that newcomers often bring. Not knowing the English language or American customs can prevent immigrants from succeeding at work or in school, and some have faced prejudice and discrimination simply because they are seen as "different."

One way government and businesses in Illinois help meet the needs of immigrant communities is by promoting businesses run by minorities. For the past few years, the state has held an event called the Heart of Illinois Trade Fair to showcase such business. In addition, national industries often hold conventions in Chicago and other Illinois cities. These conventions provide more opportunities for local minority businesses owners. At such conventions, business owners can meet other business owners in Illinois and elsewhere. Making connections like these benefits the state's economy and also strengthens feelings of community.

10 KEY EVENTS ★ ★ ★

General Grierson Liberty Days

1. Broom Corn Festival

Broomcorn, often spelled "Broom Corn," is a grass-like plant used to make brooms and brushes. Every September, the people of Arcola, the "Broom Corn Capital of the World," take to the streets for an event that includes broom-related activities and entertainment.

2. General Grierson Liberty Days

One of the largest Civil War reenactments and exhibitions in the Midwest is held every June in Jacksonville. Visitors can experience the life of a Civil War soldier, visit the Confederate and Union camps, and watch soldiers drill for battle.

3. Great Galena Balloon Race

The Great Galena Balloon Race is a three-day event featuring more than twenty hot air balloons, two races, two "night glow" extravaganzas, tethered rides, a car show, live music, and other family activities.

4. Harvard Milk Days

Harvard Milk Days is one of the longest running festivals in Illinois. This June festival brings thousands of people to Harvard to celebrate dairy farming with cattle and horse shows, an arts and crafts fair, a parade, and a carnival.

5. Illinois State Fair

Hundreds of thousands of visitors flock to the Illinois State Fairgrounds in Springfield each August for the Illinois State Fair. They enjoy ten days of entertainment including top name stars, carnival rides, food, contests, concerts, livestock shows, and auto racing.

Route 66 Mother Road festival

6. International Route 66 Mother Road Festival

More than one thousand cool cars and eighty thousand spectators roll into the heart of Springfield's historic downtown each September. This three-day celebration of cars, food, and music honors the heyday of U.S. Route 66, one of the country's most famous roads.

7. Kids Day

This gathering for children at Cahokia Mounds each May features games, storytelling, pottery making, and many other activities to honor the state's Native American heritage.

8. Magnificent Mile Lights Festival

Held in Chicago, the nation's largest evening holiday celebration kicks off the holiday season in late November with family activities, concerts by top musical artists, and a grand evening parade down Michigan Avenue illuminating one million lights on two hundred trees.

9. Superman Celebration

In June, many people gather for this annual festival in Superman's "hometown" of Metropolis to celebrate the "Man of Steel." The weekend is composed of contests, a comic book and artist show, fan films, street vendors, a carnival, costume contest, and a Super Car Show.

10. Taste of Chicago

Every summer, Chicago hosts the largest outdoor food festival in the world at Grant Park on the lakefront of Lake Michigan. Millions of people sample food from area restaurants, showcasing the diversity of Chicago's dining choices.

Magnificent Mile Lights Festival

Taste of Chicago

A statue of Abraham Lincoln greets visitors to the State Capitol in Springfield.

How the Government Works

L ike all states, Illinois has different levels of government for towns and cities, counties and the state. People in cities, towns, and villages generally elect a mayor and council members to be in charge locally. Counties usually include a number of villages, towns and sometimes a larger city. Illinois' 102 counties are divided into districts, and each district elects one supervisor (sometimes called a commissioner) to the board that governs the county.

The state government is based in Springfield, Illinois' capital city. Illinois' state government's structure is similar to the U.S. government's. It has three parts, or branches. These three branches balance each other's power.

Three State Branches

EXECUTIVE

The executive branch includes the governor, lieutenant governor, secretary of state, treasurer, comptroller and attorney general. The governor either approves or vetoes (rejects) laws passed by the legislature. The governor and other executive agencies enforce approved laws. The governor also appoints state officials and manages the state budget, which determines where the state spends its money. Governors are elected for four-year terms. Every year, the governor makes a speech called "the State of the State" address. In the speech, the governor talks about Illinois's successes and how to continue them. He or she also discusses problems affecting the state and proposes ways to fix them. The lieutenant governor assists the governor and will take over if the governor cannot complete his or her term. The secretary of state is in charge of all recordkeeping for Illinois, including drivers' licenses and other licenses. The treasurer is in charge of the investment and safekeeping of the state's money. The comptroller keeps financial

Sen. Barack Obama

Barack Obama gained national attention while serving in the Illinois Senate.

accounts for the state. The attorney general is the top lawyer for Illinois. He or she helps decide legal matters that are important to the state and its citizens.

LEGISLATIVE

The Illinois legislature, called the general assembly, makes the state's laws. The general assembly has two houses, both of which must pass a bill before it can become a law. One house, the senate, has fifty-nine members, who are elected to two-year or four-year terms. The other house, called the house of representatives, has 118 members, all of whom are elected to two-year terms.

JUDICIAL

The judicial branch contains the state's courts. Those courts apply the state's laws in specific cases and decide whether laws agree with the state constitution and are being enforced fairly.

The Illinois Supreme Court is the state's highest court. It hears cases that are appealed from lower courts. The state supreme court has seven justices. The circuit courts are the state's lower-level courts. Circuit courts hear cases that involve possible violation of state civil or criminal laws. Circuit court decisions can be appealed to a state appellate court. In Illinois, the main judges are elected for all the state's courts. However, judges in the circuit court can appoint associate judges to help them hear cases. Illinois' supreme and appellate court judges are elected for ten-year terms. Circuit court judges are elected for six-year terms. Associate judge appointments are four-year terms.

Legislators use this machine to register their votes.

Land of Many Governments

Illinois has almost seven thousand units of government—city, county, township, etc.—more than any other state. One contributing reason is the township governments, which govern areas that are generally six miles square. Texas has the second most, but it has about 1,800 fewer than Illinois.

United States Senate and Congress

Like all other states, Illinois voters chose people to represent them in the U.S. Congress in Washington, D.C. Illinois voters elect two U.S. Senators who serve six-year terms. In 2014, Illinois had eighteen representatives in the U.S. House of Representatives. Representatives serve two-year terms. A state's population determines its number of representatives.

Illinois governor Pat Quinn shows a bill he signed into law in 2009 creating a commission to fight corruption in government.

How a Bill Becomes a Law

Did you ever wonder how state laws are passed? You might be surprised to find that any citizen can get it all started.

State legislators propose laws (called bills until they are passed) to address state issues. Sometimes the ideas behind a bill come from the state's residents. If a person or a group of people think that a new law needs to be passed, they might circulate a petition. A petition is a formal written request that is signed by people who want the request carried out. The petition describes how the signers would like the state to deal with their issue. It may suggest wording for a new law. When the petition has hundreds of signatures, the people circulating the petition send it to their representatives in the Illinois house and senate.

The legislators in Springfield gauge public interest in the issue. If they receive a lot of phone calls, e-mails, letters, or petitions about it, they might work with their staff and other legislators to draft, or write, a bill. A bill is a proposal for a new law.

A bill may start out in either the house or the senate but may be changed or rejected by the other house. Each bill must be read by title on three different days in each chamber. The first reading introduces the bill. The second reading allows for amendments. When a bill is called for its third reading, it is voted on. The bill has to pass by a simple majority each time it comes up in both bodies of the legislature.

Even when both the senate and the house pass a bill, the versions that the two houses pass are not exactly the same. So senators and representatives form a committee to combine the two versions into one final bill. The new bill must again pass in both bodies of the legislature.

A bill passed by both houses must be sent to the governor within thirty days. The governor then has sixty calendar days to sign it or veto it. If the governor does nothing, the bill will automatically become a law after the sixty-day period. If the governor vetoes a bill that has been sent to him, the bill can still become law if the general assembly overrides the veto by passing the bill again by a three-fifths vote in both houses.

POLITICAL★FIGURES
FROM ILLINOIS

★ Everett Dirksen: United States Senator, 1951-1969

When President Lyndon Johnson, a Democrat, needed help passing the landmark Civil Rights Act in 1964, he got it from Republican Everett Dirksen, the Senate Minority Leader, who said: "I am involved in mankind, and whatever the skin, we are all included in mankind." Dirksen also served in the House of Representatives from 1933 to 1949.

★ Barack Obama, President of the United States, 2009-2017

Born in Hawaii in 1961, Obama began his political career in Illinois. He was elected to the Illinois state senate and, in 2004, won a seat in the U.S. Senate. In 2008, Barack Obama was elected the forty-fourth president of the United States, and was reelected in 2012.

★ Ronald Reagan: President of the United States, 1981-1989

The Dixon High School and Eureka College graduate wore many hats before being elected our fortieth president in 1980. He was a sports broadcaster and an actor, and was elected governor of California in 1966 and again in 1970.

ILLINOIS
YOU CAN MAKE A DIFFERENCE

Contacting Lawmakers

One way people get involved in politics is by contacting members of the legislature, either to give elected officials their views or to get information about what elected officials are doing.

To use any Illinois street address or zip code to find the names of the lawmakers who represent the people living in that area at the address below, visit:

www.elections.state.il.us/DistrictLocator/DistrictOfficialSearchByAddress.aspx

To find information on Illinois state senators, visit:

www.ilga.gov/senate

To find information on Illinois state representatives, visit:

www.ilga.gov/house

Half-Baked Idea

In 2014, a twelve-year-old girl named Chloe Stirling lived in Troy, Illinois. She started her own small baking business in her parents' kitchen and named it Hey Cupcake! When a local newspaper wrote a story about Chloe's business in January, the Madison County Health Department shut it down because she did not have a license or follow their health regulations.

The forced closing attracted national and international attention and criticism. Illinois state lawmakers soon stepped in. The house of representatives drafted the "Cupcake Bill" in February 2014.

The legislation quickly passed through the house and then was approved unanimously by the state senate in late May 2014. Illinois Governor Pat Quinn then traveled to the Stirling's kitchen to sign the "Cupcake Bill" into law on June 10, 2014.

The new law allows people like Chloe to legally sell baked goods, foods, or beverages made in their homes as long as they create it for themselves or on behalf of a religious, charitable or non-profit group. They also can't make more than $1,000 in sales per month.

"When all of this started, we didn't know what to do," Chloe said. "In the end, we made it work so lots of home cooks can do what they love just like me. I am really happy that a bunch of people worked together to find a solution, and I can't wait to get back to baking!"

The Illinois waterways attract tourists seeking fun.

Making a Living

Illinois' workers have many jobs, old and new. Farmers still work the land like the Native Americans and early settlers did. Factory workers still turn out equipment, following the example of early Illinois craftspeople. But Illinois is also building cutting-edge industries based on new business and technology.

Agriculture

Agriculture remains a key part of Illinois' economy. Early European American settlers found Illinois to be an excellent place for raising animals and growing crops. An article in an 1843 Illinois newspaper quoted one person who said, "Thousands of hogs was raised without any expense." Another article in the same publication spoke of "the ease with which [corn] is cultivated."

In the pioneer days, most people made their living on small farms. Today, less than one percent of Illinoisans work on farms, but the state is still the nation's second-largest producer of corn and soybeans and the fourth-largest producer of hogs. Illinois farmers provide food and food products for people in the U.S. and around the world.

Unlike the small family-run farms of long ago, today's farms are part of a highly specialized industry. Many farmers hold university degrees and use scientific and technological knowledge to make their farms as productive as possible.

★ 10 ★ KEY INDUSTRIES ★

1. Chemicals

The chemical industry in Illinois is the third largest manufacturing sector in the state. Illinois is also the fourth largest chemical producing state in the nation. The state's chemical industry ranks as Illinois' fourth largest exporter, moving $7.3 billion worth of goods out of the country in 2013.

2. Corn

Illinois' yearly harvest of more than 2.1 billion bushels makes it the country's second-largest corn producer. Most of the crop is sold as grain and livestock feed, but corn is also processed to produce corn syrup, starch and fuel, including **ethanol**.

Corn

3. Dairy Farming

Illinois dairy farms provide fresh milk, cheese, and other dairy products throughout the state and to other states as well. Illinois dairy farms produced approximately 218 million gallons of milk in 2013 and generated more than $378 million in milk sales.

Dairy

4. Financial Services

Illinois has more state-chartered banks than any other state and ranks in the top three states in the amount of total banking assets. The Chicago Mercantile Exchange (CME) is the world's second-largest trading exchange for futures and options on futures, and the largest in the United States.

5. Hogs

Farmers raise hogs for their meat, which is called pork. Ham and bacon come from hogs, as well as the sausage and pepperoni on pizzas. There are more than 4.5 million hogs in Illinois, and the state ranks fourth in U.S. pork production.

Chicago Mercantile Exchange

6. Machinery

Illinois is a leading producer of heavy machinery, including construction equipment, farm machinery, and machine tools. Caterpillar and John Deere are based in Illinois, and rank as the two largest manufacturers of construction equipment in North America. Machinery ranks as the state's number one export.

7. Service Industries

Service industries provide the largest portion of income to the Illinois economy. Personal services such as private health care, hotels, law firms, repair shops and accounting firms lead the way, with businesses in finance, insurance, and real estate coming next.

8. Soybeans

Illinois grows more soybeans than any other state, and ranks among the top soybean producers in the world. Most soybeans are used for feeding animals but they are made into products such as soy milk and tofu.

9. Technology

Illinois' technology industry continues to grow in areas like computers, Internet services, and digital publishing. Computer occupations are also by far the fastest growing group among science, technology, engineering, and math jobs.

10. Transportation

Illinois has been a center of transportation and trade since the 1850s due to its central location and its air, rail, and water facilities. Chicago's O'Hare Airport is one of the world's busiest airports.

Transportation

Soybeans

Machinery

In recent decades, many Illinois farmers who live close to a city have sold their land. Most of the time, the land is no longer used for farms. Instead, homes, businesses, and factories have been built in their place. However, in the past few years, the value of Illinois farmland has gone up dramatically. Many people realize that in addition to being important for producing food, fertile farmland can be a great investment.

Many Illinoisans who do not work directly on a farm still depend on Illinois agriculture for their jobs. Food-related industries include grain and flour milling, manufacturing food for farm animals and pets, meat processing and packing, and producing processed and packaged foods. These industries are very important to the state's economy. In fact, Chicago is one of the world's leading cities for processing, packaging, and distributing food products.

Manufacturing and Construction

Until the 1980s, thousands of Illinoisans worked in steel mills or factories that manufactured farm, construction, and industrial machinery, transportation equipment, and chemicals. However, over the past few decades, many business owners moved their

Many jobs are tied to Illinois' wheat farms, as well as the production of other agricultural products.

businesses to other countries, where labor was much cheaper, or closed their factories because their buildings and equipment were old and the cost of replacing them was too high. When manufacturing plants closed in Illinois, many people lost their jobs.

Even so, both manufacturing and construction remain very important industries in Illinois. In addition to food manufacturing industries, Illinois is home to many other manufacturing businesses, which create a wide variety of products. Some companies make heavy machinery. Others make chemicals, medicine, and medical instruments, electronics, computers, and computer parts, and objects from cement, concrete, and recycled steel that are used in the construction industry. The state also has paper mills, printers, and publishers. Some companies make medicines, and others make medical instruments. Still, Illinois's biggest manufacturing industry is the chemical industry. Among other products, Illinois chemical manufacturers make fertilizers, ethanol (an automobile fuel), and even chemicals for cleaning polluted water. With all these different kinds of factories, Illinois ranked fourth in the nation in 2012 in number of manufacturing jobs.

Ford's Chicago Assembly Plant puts people to work.

Caramel Popcorn

Popcorn is the official Illinois state snack food. More than three hundred Illinois farms grow popping corn on 47,000 acres (19 ha), making the state the third largest grower of popping corn in the United States. Popcorn pops because its kernel contains a small drop of water that suddenly expands when exposed to high heat. The kernel turns inside out as it explodes.

What You Need

1/2 gallon (1.9 liters) prepared popcorn

2 cups (473 grams) brown sugar

1 cup (237 g) butter

1/2 cup (118 milliliters) corn syrup or 1/2 cup (118 mL) maple syrup

1/2 teaspoon (2.5 mL) baking soda

1/2 teaspoon (2.5 mL) salt

1 teaspoon (5 mL) vanilla

1 cup (237 g) peanuts (Optional)

What to Do

1. Preheat oven to 250°F (121°C).

2. Prepare popcorn and set aside.

3. In a saucepan bring to a boil brown sugar, butter, and syrup.

4. Cook at a slow boil for five minutes without stirring.

5. Remove from heat and add baking soda, salt, vanilla, and peanuts.

6. Pour over popcorn and toss.

7. Lay out on greased cookie sheets and bake for one hour, stirring every twenty minutes.

8. Store in large, resealable sandwich bags.

Health, Educational, and Social Services

More than half of Illinois workers are employed in a service industry. Service industries are those whose main business is helping people: hospitals, schools, insurance agencies, governmental agencies, banks and other financial institutions, hotels, retail stores, and restaurants are a few examples.

Finance

Chicago is the financial center of the Midwest. In fact, the U.S. government has a bank there: the Federal Reserve Bank of Chicago. The Chicago Mercantile Exchange and the Chicago Board of Options Exchange play important roles in worldwide investment.

Chicago, along with other cities in Illinois, helps make the state a center for wholesale and retail trade. The state's central location and its strong transportation system help link Illinois to the rest of the country and the world.

Sports

Illinois' professional sports teams bring a lot of money to the state. Chicago has two famous Major League Baseball teams, the Cubs and the White Sox. The Chicago Blackhawks are one of the original six teams in the National Hockey League. The city's football and basketball teams, the Bears (NFL), the Bulls (NBA) and the Sky (WNBA), have fans all over the country. The Chicago Fire, a Major League Soccer team, also has a loyal following. In addition, fans of auto racing flock to Chicagoland Speedway in Joliet to watch their favorite NASCAR and IndyCar drivers.

Tourism

Tourists come from all over the world to see everything that Illinois has to offer. They may want to see the bustling city of Chicago, the beautiful blue waters of Lake Michigan, or the wilderness in Shawnee National Forest. Tourists and residents alike enjoy kayaking, rock climbing, fishing, and camping in Illinois' many and varied state parks and natural areas. The money that tourists spend in hotels, restaurants, and shops helps boost the economy of the Prairie State.

Education

Education is very important in Illinois—and a big part of the economy. As of 2014, the state had close to 5,500 elementary and secondary schools and more than 2.1 million students in grades pre-K through twelve. Public and nonpublic schools in the state employ about 200,000 people.

Researchers from the prestigious University of Chicago use the particle accelerator in Batavia.

The University of Illinois has campuses in Chicago, Springfield, and Urbana-Champaign. More than seventy thousand students are enrolled on the three campuses, and thousands more take classes off campus and online. Illinois operates nine other public universities that are scattered throughout the state.

Illinois also has many fine private colleges and universities. The University of Chicago is one of the leading research centers in the country. Some of the top scholars and scientists in the world have taught at or attended the university. U.S. President Barack Obama was a professor at the University of Chicago Law School before he was elected to the U.S. Senate. Northwestern University in Evanston is another private university with a top reputation throughout the country. Its graduates include many well-known politicians, business leaders, entertainers, and journalists.

Energy

Illinois needs a lot of electricity to power its homes and businesses. However, electricity production is important in Illinois for another reason. The state makes money by exporting some of the electricity it generates to other states. Today, coal and nuclear power plants provide most of the electricity generated in Illinois. However, burning coal can pollute the atmosphere and the nuclear power plants in Illinois and across the country are several decades old. They will need to be rebuilt or replaced soon. The state of Illinois is looking at new ways to provide energy.

In recent years, scientists have developed new technologies related to burning coal. Using these technologies, factories and power plants that burn coal can lessen their emissions and help coal-burning power plants become safer and more efficient.

Illinoisans know that it is important to protect the air we breathe, the water we drink, our natural resources, and our wildlife. The state has developed many programs to encourage people to protect the environment. Some of these programs encourage the use of renewable energy sources, such as solar and wind power.

Illinois has a program to help people learn about wind energy. The state makes maps that show people how windy it is where they live. They can use the maps to decide whether installing a wind turbine would help them save money on their electricity bill. People who produce more electricity than they use might even be able to make money by selling their extra electricity back to one of Illinois's power companies.

Most schools in Illinois have special environmental awareness programs. Earth Day in the Park is held at state parks around Illinois each spring. Students at these events may plant trees, restore a local prairie, or even help build a butterfly garden. They enjoy coming back later in the year to see how their project has helped the environment.

Looking to the Future

Illinois will continue to grow and change. New industries will replace old ones. Cities will grow and change as populations shift. The spirit of its people, and their ability to adapt, has helped Illinois get through difficult times. Its proud people are ready to face the future. It is their enthusiasm that has kept the Prairie State alive and well.

Illinois is seeking new ways to meet its energy needs.

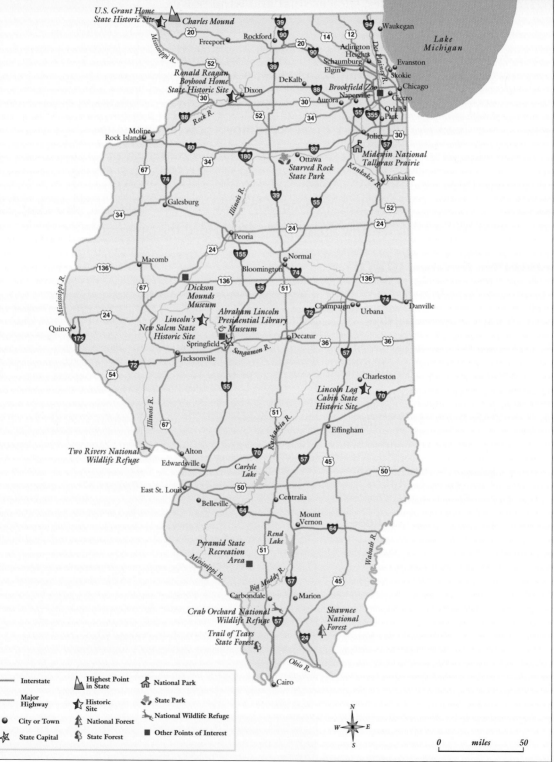

U.S. Grant Home
State Historic Site
Charles Mound

Mississippi R.

20
Freeport
Rockford
39
90
14
12
94
Waukegan

Lake
Michigan

Arlington
Heights
Schaumburg
Elgin
Evanston
Skokie

52
Ronald Reagan
Boyhood Home
State Historic Site
Dixon
DeKalb
88
Brookfield Zoo
Naperville
Chicago
Cicero

39
90
20

30
Moline
Rock Island
Rock R.
88
52
30
Aurora
34
55
355
Orland
Park
Joliet
30

80
80
Ottawa
Starved Rock
State Park
Midewin National
Tallgrass Prairie
57

67
180
39
Kankakee R.
Kankakee

74
55

34
52
34

Galesburg
24
24

Illinois R.
Peoria

136
Macomb
24
155
Normal
Bloomington
74
136

67
Dickson
Mounds
Museum
136
55
51
Champaign
Urbana
74
Danville

24
Lincoln's
New Salem State
Historic Site
Abraham Lincoln
Presidential Library
& Museum
72
Decatur
36
36

Quincy
172

54
72
Jacksonville
Springfield
Sangamon R.
57

Illinois R.
55
Charleston
Lincoln Log
Cabin State
Historic Site
70

67
51
Kaskaskia R.
Effingham

Two Rivers National
Wildlife Refuge
Alton
70
57
45
50
Edwardsville
Carlyle
Lake

East St. Louis
50
Centralia

Belleville
64
Mount
Vernon
64

Pyramid State
Recreation
Area
Rend
Lake
51
Mississippi R.
Big Muddy R.
Wabash R.

Carbondale
57
Marion
Shawnee
National
Forest
45

Crab Orchard National
Wildlife Refuge
57
Trail of Tears
State Forest
24

Ohio R.
Cairo

Legend:

—	Interstate
—	Major Highway
●	City or Town
☆	State Capital
▲	Highest Point in State
★	Historic Site
🌲	National Forest
🌲	State Forest
⌂	National Park
🦌	State Park
🦌	National Wildlife Refuge
■	Other Points of Interest

N
W   E
S

0   miles   50

★ ILLINOIS
MAP SKILLS

1. The Kaskaskia River feeds what lake?

2. Starved Rock State Park is located close to what city?

3. How many different interstate highways are in Illinois?

4. What Illinois town or city is furthest south on the map?

5. What is the highest point in Illinois?

6. What river runs the length of the western Illinois border?

7. What town or city on the map is located closest to Pyramid State Recreation Area?

8. The U.S. Grant Home State Historic Site is located in what corner of Illinois (Northeast, Northwest, Southeast, or Southwest)?

9. What three Illinois cities are on the shore of Lake Michigan?

10. What interstate would you take to drive from Chicago south to Marion?

Mississippi River

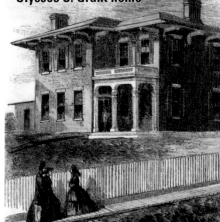

Ulysses S. Grant home

10. Interstate 57
9. Chicago, Evanston, and Waukegan
8. Northwest
7. Carbondale
6. Mississippi River
5. Charles Mound
4. Cairo
3. Sixteen (Routes 24, 39, 55, 57, 64, 70, 72, 74, 80, 88, 90, 94, 155, 172, 180, 355)
2. Ottawa
1. Carlyle Lake

State Flag, Seal, and Song

Illinois' flag shows the state seal on a white background.

The state seal has a bald eagle holding a shield with the stars and stripes that represent the thirteen original states. In its beak, the eagle holds a banner with the state's motto—*State Sovereignty, National Union.* The eagle is perched on a boulder that shows the year the state entered the Union (1818) and the year this version of the seal was adopted (1868).

The state song is "Illinois," with words by C.H. Chamberlain and music by Archibald Johnston.

To learn the lyrics, visit

www.illinois.gov/about/Pages/StateSong.aspx

ILLINOIS

Glossary

artifact	An object made by a human being, typically of cultural or historical interest.
assassinated	Killed for political or ideological reasons; the victim is usually prominent.
Cahokia	The city where a great civilization of Mississippian peoples thrived long before European settlers came to America.
Chicagoland	An informal name used to describe the city of Chicago and its surrounding suburbs. Depending on the user, the term sometimes includes eight nearby Illinois counties as well as parts of Indiana and Wisconsin.
ethanol	A grain alcohol that can be blended with gasoline and used in motor vehicles. Most of the ethanol made in the United States comes from corn grown in the Midwest.
Great Depression	A period of severe worldwide economic decline that took place in the decade (1930s) just before World War II.
Great Lakes	A group of five freshwater lakes of central North America between the United States and Canada, including lakes Superior, Huron, Erie, Ontario, and Michigan.
immigrants	People who leave one country and come to another to live there.
mounds	Earth piled onto rounded hills on which Cahokians constructed temples, government buildings, and homes of their leaders.
National Organization for Women [NOW]	The largest organization of feminist activists in the United States.
nomadic	Anything that moves around a lot, usually referring to hunter-gatherer tribes that follow the animals they hunt.
nuclear	Relating to the nucleus of the atom, or to something powered by nuclear energy, which is used to generate heat for producing steam, which is used by a turbine to generate electricity.
reservations	The areas of land given to Native Americans by the U.S. government.

More About Illinois

BOOKS

Horn, Geoffrey M. *Barack Obama*. Pleasantville, NY: Gareth Stevens, 2009.

Murphy, Jim. *The Great Fire*. New York, NY: Scholastic Paperbacks, 2010.

Obama, Barack. *Of Thee I Sing: A Letter to My Daughters*. New York, NY: Alfred A Knopf, 2010.

Russell, Herbert K. *The State of Southern Illinois: An Illustrated History*. Carbondale, IL: Southern Illinois University Press, 2012.

WEBSITES

Illinois State Historical Library:
www.state.il.us/HPA/PrairiePages.htm

Official Illinois State Website:
www.illinois.gov/Pages/default.aspx

Official Illinois State Tourism Website:
www.enjoyillinois.com

ABOUT THE AUTHOR

Claire Price-Groff is the author of several books for young adults. She particularly loves writing about history and the people who made it.

Elizabeth Kaplan has edited textbooks and reference works on a wide variety of subjects. She is also the author of several science and social studies books for young adults.

Gerry Boehme is an author, speaker, and business consultant who was born in New York City.

Index

Page numbers in **boldface** are illustrations.

Index